220 Chinese Proverbs To Make You Instantly Wiser

George Tam

ISBN: 1 5 1 7 0 8 8 3 9 9

ISBN-13: 9 7 8 - 1 5 1 7 0 8 8 3 9 2

CONTENTS

1. VISION

视力

In every crisis, there is opportunity.

To see things in the seed- that is genius.

Vision without action is a daydream. Action without vision is a nightmare.

People who say it cannot be done should not interrupt those who are doing it.

Learn from yesterday. Live for today. Hope for tomorrow.

2. PURPOSE

Be not afraid of growing slowly. Be afraid only of standing still.

There are many paths to the top of the mountain, but the view is the same.

Often one finds one's destiny just where one hides to avoid it.

Find a job you love and you'll never work a day in your life.

Wherever you go, go with all your heart.

3. SELF

You discover who you are by acting naturally.

The snow goose need not bathe to make itself white. Neither need you do anything but be yourself.

Tension is who you think you should be. Relaxation is who you are.

When you are content to be simply yourself and don't compare or compete, everybody will respect you.

We are fools whether we dance or not, so we might as well dance.

Care about what other people think and you will always be their prisoner.

A wise man makes his own decisions. Ignorant man follows public opinions.

4. AMBITION

Falling hurts least for those who fly low.

If you shoot for the stars and hit the moon, that's all right. But you've got to shoot for something. A lot of people don't even shoot.

By filling one's head instead of one's pocket, one cannot be robbed.

He who sacrifices his conscience to ambition burns a picture to obtain the ashes.

Great souls have wills; feeble ones have only wishes.

5. KNOWLEDGE

Learning is a treasure that will follow its owner everywhere.

A book is like a garden carried in a pocket.

A book tightly shut is but a block of paper.

Your teacher can open the door, but you must enter by yourself.

Tell me and I'll forget.

Show me, and I may remember.

Involve me, and I will understand.

Give a man a fish and you feed him a day. Teach a man to fish and you feed him a lifetime.

He who asks is a fool for five minutes, but who does not ask is a fool forever.

Life is finite but knowledge is infinite.

Learn as though you would never be able to master it.

To learn a language is to have one more window from which to look at the world.

A nation's treasure is in its scholars.

6. EXPERIENCE

经验

Reading a thousand books is not as useful as travelling ten thousand miles.

A single conversation with a wise man is worth a month's study of books.

To know the road ahead, ask those coming back.

By three methods we may learn wisdom: First, by reflection, which is the noblest; Second, by imitation, which is easiest; and third, by experience, which is the bitterest.

Experience is a comb which nature gives to men when they are bald.

7. STRENGTH

强度

A single arrow is easily broken, but not ten in a bundle.

He who controls others may be powerful, but he who has mastered himself is mightier.

Knowing others is intelligence;

Knowing yourself is true wisdom.

Mastering others is strength;

Mastering yourself is true power.

If you realize that you have enough,

You are truly rich.

8. JOURNEY

旅程

A journey of a thousand miles begins with a single step.

Pearls don't lie on the seashore. If you want one, you must dive for it.

A trail through the mountains, if used, becomes a path in short time, but misused, becomes blocked by grass in an equally short time.

The loftiest towers rise from the ground.

The man who removes a mountain begins by carrying away small stones.

Journey is the reward.

9. BALANCE

*With money you can buy a house,
but not a home.*

*With money you can buy a clock, but
not time.*

*With money you can buy a bed, but
not sleep.*

*With money you can buy a book, but
not knowledge.*

*With money you can buy a doctor,
but not good health.*

*With money you can buy a position,
but not respect.*

*With money you can buy blood, but
not life.*

With money you can buy sex, but not love.

If there is light in the soul, there will be beauty in the person.

If there is beauty in the person, there will be harmony in the house.

If there is harmony in the house, there will be order in the nation.

If there is order in the nation, there will be peace in the world.

A man who chases two rabbits catches neither.

Fill your bowl to the brim and it will spill. Keep sharpening your knife and it will blunt.

He who knows that enough is enough will always have enough.

10. ADAPTING

Life is a series of natural and spontaneous changes. Don't resist them. That only creates sorrow. Let reality be reality. Let things flow naturally forward in whatever way they like.

The wise adapt themselves to circumstances, as water molds itself to the pitcher.

When the wind change blows, some build walls, while others build windmills.

A good traveler has no fixed plans and is not intent on arriving.

11. HABITS

Sow a thought, reap an action;

Sow an action, reap a habit;

Sow a habit, reap a character;

Sow a character, reap a destiny.

Habits are cobwebs at first, cables at last.

Be the first to the field and the last to the couch.

Defer not until tomorrow what may be done today.

If a thing's worth doing, it's worth doing well.

12. PREPARATION

Failing to plan is planning to fail.

A drop of sweat spent in a drill is a drop of blood saved in a battle.

Sow much, reap much.
Sow little, reap little.

Raise your sail one foot and you get ten feet of wind.

Like weather, one's fortune may change by the evening.

Dig the well before you are thirsty.

13. MINDFULNESS

Of a good beginning cometh a good end.

Men trip not on mountains. They trip on molehills.

A minimal error at the start leads to a wide convergence in the distance.

14. TRUTH

The beginning of wisdom is to call things by their rightful names.

Truthful words are not beautiful;

beautiful words are not truthful.

Good words are not persuasive; Persuasive words are not good.

The more you try to cover things up, the more exposed they will be.

A lie has many variations, truth none.

15. ACTION

If you do not change direction, you will end up where you are going.

When it is obvious that the goals cannot be reached, don't adjust the goals. Adjust the action steps.

The best time to plant a tree was twenty years ago. The second best time is now.

Always leave a little room a mistake.

16. DIFFICULTY

If your mind is strong, all difficult things will be easy; if your mind is weak, all easy things will become difficult.

A clever person turns great troubles into little ones and little ones into none at all.

All things seem difficult at first.

To get through the hardest journey, we need take only one step at a time, but we must keep stepping.

17. PERSISTENCE

坚持

A gem cannot be polished without carving and polishing, nor a man perfected without trials.

Distance tests a horse's strength. Time reveals a person's character.

The temptation to quit will be greatest just before you are about to succeed.

18. PATIENCE

A little impatience will spoil great plans.

With time and patience, the mulberry leaf becomes a silk gown.

You won't help the new plants grow by pulling them up higher.

A melon forced off its vine is not sweet.

Nature does not hurry, yet everything is accomplished.

19. WORRY

To the mind that is still, the whole universe surrenders.

If your problem has a solution, then why worry about it?

If your problem doesn't have a solution, then why worry about it?

Don't count the chickens before they are hatched.

When you have two pennies left in the world, buy a loaf of bread with one and a lily with the other.

Do not anxiously hope for that which is not yet come. Do not vainly regret what is already passed.

Shed no tears until seeing the coffin.

20. FAILURE

失败

Failure is the mother of success.

Failure is not falling, but refusing to get up.

Our greatest glory is not in never falling, but in rising every time we fall.

The longer the night lasts, the more dreams we'll have.

21. ANGER

愤怒

A bad workman blames his tools.

If you are patient in one moment of anger, you will escape a hundred days of sorrow.

When anger rises, think of the consequences.

Respond intelligently even to unintelligent treatment.

If you don't want anyone to find out, don't do it.

Clear conscience never fears midnight knocking.

If you stand straight, do not fear a crooked shadow.

22. CONFLICT

A friend made is a road paved; an enemy created is a wall built.

A thousand cups of wine do not suffice when true friends meet, but half a sentence is too much when there is no meeting of the minds.

Quarreling is like cutting water with a sword.

One never needs their humor as much as when they argue with a fool.

He who strikes the first blow admits he's lost an argument.

Keep your broken arm inside your sleeve.

Kill one to warn a hundred.

Dismantle the bridge after crossing it.

The one who pursues revenge should dig two graves.

The fire you kindle in your enemy often burns yourself more than him.

23. ACCEPTANCE

验收

Tears cannot put out a fire.

Water spilled can never be retrieved.

You cannot prevent the birds of sadness from passing over your head, but you can prevent their making a nest in your hair.

24. MOVING FORWARD

Don't stand by the water and long for fish; go home and weave a net.

Better to light one small candle than to curse the darkness.

Write injuries in sand, kindness in marble.

25. TRANSFORMATION

If you survived a storm, you won't be bothered by the rain.

Out of the hottest fire comes the strongest steel.

He who returns from a journey is not the same as he who left.

26. GRATITUDE

We count our miseries carefully and accept our blessing without much thought.

Be content with what you have; rejoice in the way things are. When you realize there is nothing lacking, the whole world belongs to you.

I was angry that I had no shoes. Then I met a man with no feet.

The palest ink is better than the best memory.

27. SIMPLICITY

Life is simple, but we insist on making it complicated.

Blessed are those who can laugh at themselves. They shall never cease to be entertained.

Everyone eats and drinks, yet only few appreciate the taste of food.

Don't take life so seriously. It's not like you're going to get out alive.

Enjoy yourself. It's later than you think.

28. FRIENDSHIP

An invisible red thread connects those who are destined to meet regardless of time, place, or circumstance. The thread may stretch or tangle but it will never break.

Fate brings people together no matter how far apart they may be.

Life is partly what we make it and partly what it is made by friends whom we choose.

Friends are siblings God never gave us.

Friends are known first in hardships.

29. CRITICISM

It takes little effort to watch a man carry a load.

The wound caused by a sword can eventually be healed; the hurt resulted from vicious remarks can never be undone.

Deal with faults of others as gently with your own.

Once bitten by a snake, one is scared all his life at the mere sight of a rope.

Do not remove a fly from your friend's forehead with a hatchet.

30. KINDNESS

Life is an echo. What you send out comes back.

Behave toward everyone as if receiving a guest.

Make happy those who are near and those who are far will come.

Keep a green tree in your heart and perhaps a singing bird will come.

Do not impose on others what you yourself do not desire.

Great acts are made up of small deeds.

If you always give, you will always have.

He who obtains has little. He who scatters has much.

One happiness scatters a thousand sorrows.

Without sorrows, no one becomes saint.

Thousands of candles can be lit from a single candle, and the candle will never be shorted. Happiness never decreases by being shared.

A bit of fragrance clings to the hand that gives flowers.

31. HAPPINESS

If you want happiness for an hour, take a nap.

If you want happiness for a day, go fishing.

If you want happiness for a month, get married.

If you want happiness for a year, inherit a fortune.

If you want happiness for a lifetime, help someone else.

A life with love is happy; a life for love is foolish.

Being deeply loved by someone gives you strength, while loving someone gives you courage.

32. PEOPLE

A person cannot be judged by his appearance in the same token as the sea cannot be measured with a bucket.

A diamond with a flaw is worth more than a pebble without perfection.

A speck on a jade stone won't obscure its radiance.

There are two kinds of perfect people; those who are dead and those who have not been born yet.

If heaven made him, earth can find some use for him.

A fool judges people by the presents they give him.

If you wish to know the mind of a man, listen to his words.

The one who understands does not speak; the one who speaks does not understand.

Those who have knowledge don't predict. Those who predict don't have knowledge.

The longer the explanation, the bigger the lie.

Don't listen to what they say, go see.

Fool me once, shame on you; fool me twice, shame on me.

He who knows not and not knows he knows not- he is fool. Shun him.

He who knows not and knows he knows not- he is simple. Teach him.

He who knows and knows not he knows- he is asleep. Wake him.

He who knows and knows he knows- he is wise. Follow him.

A flying moth throws itself into the fire.

If I am walking with two other men, each of them will serve as my teacher. I will pick out the good points of the one and imitate them, and the bad points of the other and correct them in myself.

He who is drowned is not troubled by the rain.

A dog will jump over a wall when cornered.

One dog snarls at a shadow; a hundred howl at each other barking.

What is told into the ear of a man is often heard a hundred miles away.

Your friend has a friend; don't tell him.

Do not employ handsome servants.

Don't suspect someone you employ, but if one is suspicious, don't employ him.

A base person often thinks of a man of honor as mean as himself.

A tiger never returns to his prey he did not finish off.

Paper can't wrap up a fire.

33. LEADERSHIP

The greatest conqueror is he who overcomes the enemy without a blow.

A leader is best when people barely know he exists. When his work is done, his aim fulfilled, they will say, "We did it ourselves."

To lead people, walk behind them.

The softest things in the world overcome the hardest things in the world.

34. SUPERIORITY

The superior man is modest in his speech, but exceeds in his actions.

The superior man is distressed by the limitations of his ability; he is not distressed by the fact that men do not recognize the ability that he has.

The superior doctor prevents sickness.

The mediocre doctor attends to impending sickness.

The inferior doctor treats actual sickness.

35. PERSPECTIVE

A spectator sees more than a player in the heat of a game.

A fly before his own eye is bigger than an elephant in the next field.

To enjoy a grander sight, climb to a greater height.

The nail that sticks out gets hammered down.

In the midst of great joy, do not promise anything. In the midst of great anger, do not answer anyone's letter.

Distant water won't help to put out a fire close at hand.

Cheap things are not good; good things are not cheap.

Silence is a true friend who never betrays.

Once on a tiger's back, you'll find it hard to get off.

At birth we bring nothing; at death we leave the same.

Not only can water float a boat, it can also sink it.

Too many cooks spoil the broth.

It is the beautiful bird that gets caged.

36. FAMILY

There is only one pretty child in the world... and every mother has it.

A child's life is like a piece of paper on which every person leaves a mark.

A bird does not sing because it has an answer. It sings because it has a song.

Do not confine your children to your own learning, for they were born in another time.

Parents who are afraid to put their foot down usually have kids who step on their toes.

Reward and punishments are the lowest from of education.

A family in harmony will prosper in everything.

In a broken nest there are few whole eggs.

Each generation will reap what the former generation has sown.

One generation plants the tree. Another gets the shade.

To forget one's ancestors is to be a brook without a source, a tree without root.

Falling leaves return to their roots.

To understand your parents' love, you must raise children yourself.

Respect for one's parents is the highest duty of civil life.

Printed in Great Britain
by Amazon